vOUCHers

Learn more at www.OUCHer.net

Many thanks to all of those who helped us bring this book to life.
With special appreciation to Oz, Evie, Poppy, Mike, Elizabeth,
Lorraine and Laura for their support and feedback.

The advice and information provided in this book is for general help and guidance only and anyone at all unsure of how to deal with a specific problem should consult an appropriate professional. We do our utmost to bring you relevant and reliable information, but we can take no responsibility for any advice offered.

The book is not, necessarily, endorsed or supported by any charities that appear in this book. Their names, brands and their logos are shown for your reference only.

This book has been created to share the work of the author(s) and has not been designed to be upsetting or offensive in any way.

vOUCHers

Jennifer Dunning & Mark 'Markus' Baker

Published by R-and-Q.com.

ISBN: 978-1-9163571-2-9

vOUCHers

The idea for the vOUCHers stemmed from a simple conversation with my 10 year old. At the start of the 2020 lockdown, I spent time talking through Internet safety with my children aged 10 and seven. Building on their school's teaching, I thought I'd nailed it, ready for the online learning that was to follow. For three weeks all seemed well, until one night my eldest, as I tucked her up in bed as I routinely did every night, announced that she had something to tell me. Her look was of fear, her words shaky. All sorts went through my mind. "Go on," I said, "I'm listening." She took a deep breath.

"Mum, I went on a website I shouldn't have." I gave her silence and space to allow her to tell me more. She went onto explain that she'd accidentally clicked on a pop up site. I was relieved that as she told me, it transpired to be an innocent site. No harm done.

"Are you mad at me, Mum?" I hugged her and said no, and that I was pleased that she'd told me. It clearly bothered her. "When did this happen?" I asked. Last week she said, "But I was afraid to tell you because you'd told us the rules of being online and I broke them. I thought you'd be angry."

This had worried her all week she said. She'd tried a few times to pluck up the courage – and I had no idea.

This led me to think. If my own daughter held this very simple and in fact, a very innocent fear from an action that in this case led her to no danger, what of others who have similar secrets, or indeed secrets of a grander, more serious scale. Potentially of trauma, fear and real danger, but who dare not tell anyone.

Having worked in children's homes, as a class teacher and a special educational needs coordinator in school, and now more recently as a specialist teacher with an additional role of leading academic progress of children in care for an authority, I am fully aware of secrets that can be both small and innocent or be huge and trauma inflicting. How many are kept through fear because the person either does not get that chance to tell or does not have the space to disclose. So the idea of allowing any person the opportunity to tell a trusted person, without the initial use of verbal communication, that they want time to talk. To ask that someone not to judge but be there. Small or big, a chance to talk about what is happening or has happened no matter what it is. To allow the chance for them to talk without the fear of the other person telling them off. To feel that they have space and support. So they feel that they are no longer alone.

It was at this point I decided to speak to Mark, a fellow Samaritans listening volunteer at Boston Branch and an experienced graphic designer, who has worked for the film industry and currently writes and illustrates both fictional children's picture books as well as factual books. I shared the idea of a coupon type book that could help everybody get the emotional support they feel they need. Mark, loving the idea, felt we should name the project vOUCHers, which I felt was a great idea. He then set about creating the visual identity and style. We then, between us, wrote the book, with me creating the vOUCHers and Mark the introductions to each section.

This all resulted in what you see before you today, unique vOUCHers that asks the receiver something special. And the chance for the giver to be listened to in a safe space. We hope that by gifting this book to some you care about you are telling the receiver: "I am here for you. No matter what you tell me."

Mark and I both hope this book and its supporting website will give everybody the opportunity to talk, feel listened to in a safe environment, where time and no judgement is provided. Therefore, fulling its purpose of providing support for any pain that is caused by an emotional OUCH!

Jennifer

September 2020

Welcome to vOUCHers

For those times when you are hurting emotionally, these vOUCHers can help you find the support that you need.

Choose the vOUCHer and a person that you feel would support you best.

Then cut the vOUCHer out from this book, write yours and their name on the back. Then, either, give it to them in person or leave it somewhere that you know they will find it.

> *Don't be shy about asking for help. It doesn't mean you're weak, it only means you're wise.*

The Japanese way of vOUCHers

Although we have no specific links with Japan, there are a few points from their culture that we would like to share that may be of help when using the vOUCHers.

Kintsukuroi is when a broken pot is repaired with gold. The repaired cracks, just like us after we have fixed our issues, can be even more precious than before. Using these vOUCHers and working our way through our tough times can help us feel more connected and special than before our issues arose.

Objects, even small ones, are given with two hands, this is to demonstrate the importance and high value of the object being given. You may wish to hand over your vOUCHer with two hands.

Origami, the Japanese art of paper folding, has been said to be a great way of helping manage stress. Engaging both the mind and hands can be very calming. Each vOUCHer has been designed to be folded into an envelope. You can follow the instructions on how to do this at www.oucher.net/voucher-folding/

How are you feeling?

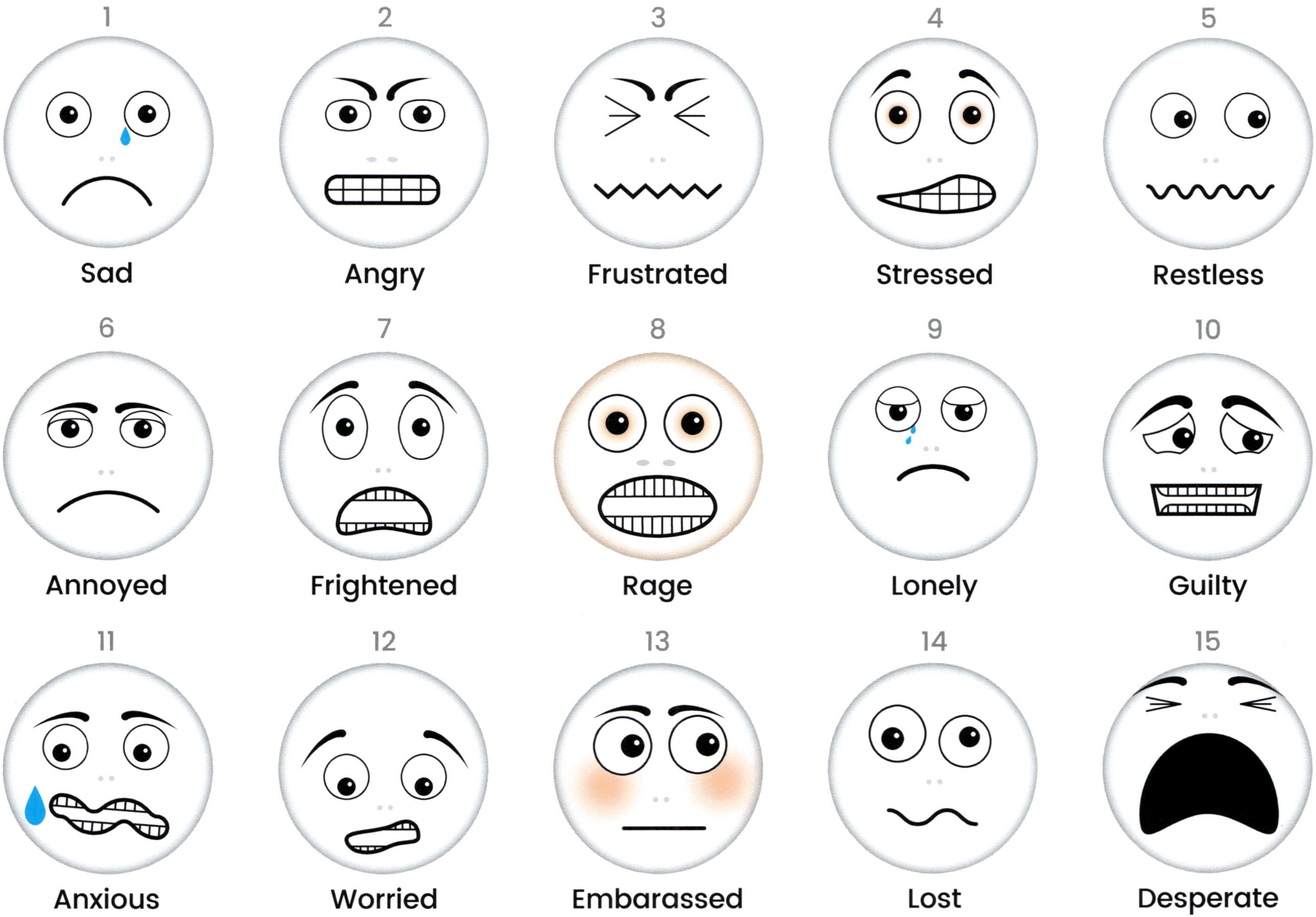

Have we missed any feelings?

If so, please draw below and label it with the emotion.

16

17

18

19

20

21

22

23

24

25

26

27

28

29

30

A friendly listening ear

How being listened to can help

When listened to properly we can feel connected because the person has empathised with us. They really try to stand in our shoes and see the world through our eyes.

By listening and not telling you what to do leaves you with the space to discover the best option for you.

Finally, by sharing your story, feelings and thoughts you can help lift the weight off your shoulders.

"A problem shared is a problem halved."

#1 Replacement password: 730172

VOUCH!

This voucher asks that the receiver listens to me without telling me off.

I did wrong, I know I did wrong and I have learned from it, but I want to tell you about it.

VOUCH!

This voucher asks that the receiver listens to me without telling me off.

I did wrong, I know I did wrong and I have learned from it, but I want to tell you about it.

To:

vOUCHer

From:

www.OUCHer.net

To:

vOUCHer

From:

www.OUCHer.net

A Hug

How a hug can help

Did you know that when two people hug it is the closest their two hearts can ever be? A hug demonstrates that the two people want to connect on a heart to heart level.

Studies have shown that hugs help reduce stress, fear and pain.

When we hug, our bodies can release the “cuddle hormone” called Oxytocin which is the chemical that is linked to increasing happiness.

> *I have learned that there is more power in a good strong hug than in a thousand meaningful words.*
>
> Ann Hood

#2 Replacement password: 692691

VOUCH!

This voucher asks that the receiver gives me a hug because:

a. I need one, please don't ask me why
b. I need one, please ask me why
c. I need one, I am not sure I have the words to explain
d. You need one

VOUCH!

This voucher asks that the receiver gives me a hug because:

a. I need one, please don't ask me why
b. I need one, please ask me why
c. I need one, I am not sure I have the words to explain
d. You need one

To:

vOUCHer

From:

www.OUCHer.net

To:

vOUCHer

From:

www.OUCHer.net

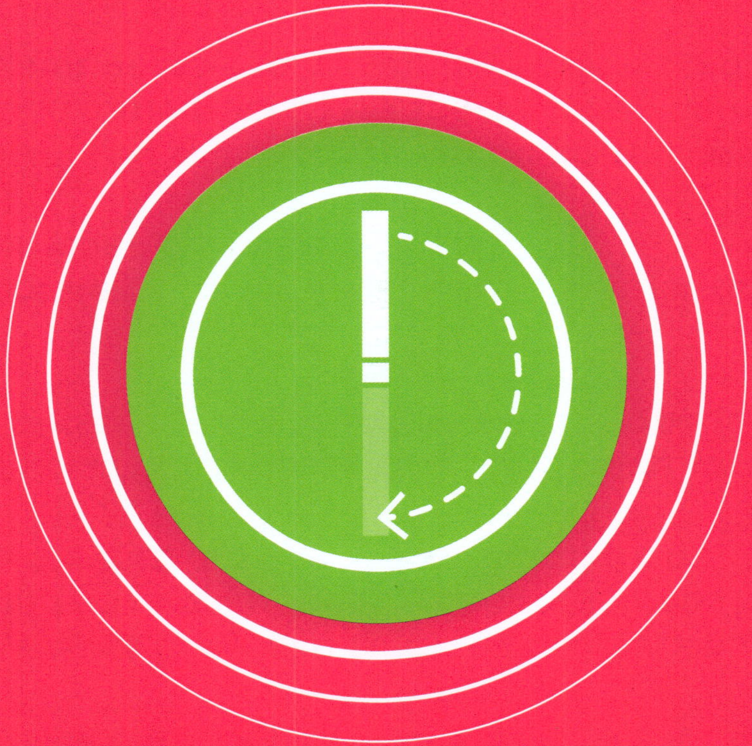

A moment of your time

How sharing a moment can help

In a world where we are busy with so many distractions like our devices, social media, tv and advertising, people can sometimes forget to prioritise the things in their life that are truly important to them.

Stopping and consciously choosing to set time aside, maybe on a regular basis, to connect and ensure we see those we care about most is of benefit to both parties.

Sharing a moment helps us to feel valued, cared for and that we are a special part of someone else's life.

Memories that are linked with stronger emotions are easier to remember which is why we can remember those special times and big events in our lives though may not be able to remember what we did last Tuesday.

"*Time is the most valuable thing a person can spend.*"

Theophrastus

#3 Replacement password: 468265

VOUCH!

This voucher asks that the receiver gives me half an hour of their undivided attention to:

a. Talk with me about my day, it's been ______________________________
b. Listen to me talk about my day without comment or judgement, it's been ______________________________
c. Sit with me, I just need you to be near
d. Tell me about your day

VOUCH!

This voucher asks that the receiver gives me half an hour of their undivided attention to:

a. Talk with me about my day, it's been ______________________________
b. Listen to me talk about my day without comment or judgement, it's been ______________________________
c. Sit with me, I just need you to be near
d. Tell me about your day

To:

vOUCHer

From:

www.OUCHer.net

To:

vOUCHer

From:

www.OUCHer.net

Listen then speak

How listening to advice can help

Sometimes when we are anxious, stressed or feeling down, the emotions can make it difficult to think clearly and logically.

Scientists at the University of Pittsburgh discovered that negative emotions like anxiety can hinder us in making the best choices for our lives.

Seeking advice from someone you trust can help you think more clearly. It may also help you to find your own solutions.

Remember, it is your life and you can choose whether or not to take the advice you are given.

> *All the advice in the world will never help you until you help yourself*
>
> Fred Van Amburgh

#4 Replacement password: 210836

VOUCH!

This voucher asks that the receiver listens and gives me advice without telling me off or getting angry about what I am going to say.

VOUCH!

This voucher asks that the receiver listens and gives me advice without telling me off or getting angry about what I am going to say.

To:

vOUCHer

From:

www.OUCHer.net

To:

vOUCHer

From:

www.OUCHer.net

Undivided Attention

How being given undivided attention can help

Having the undivided attention of someone else is powerful because it shows that you are cared about.

We can lack focus with screens, people and problems all vying for our attention.

When we consciously choose to give somebody our full attention, a real connection can happen that can help both the giver and receiver feel calmer and less stressed.

> *The greatest gift you can give anyone is your undivided attention.*
>
> Will Schwalbe

VOUCH!

This voucher asks the receiver to give me their undivided attention to:

a. Watch a film
b. Have a drink and chat
c. Read together
d. Play a game or do puzzles

VOUCH!

This voucher asks the receiver to give me their undivided attention to:

a. Watch a film
b. Have a drink and chat
c. Read together
d. Play a game or do puzzles

To:

vOUCHer

From:

www.OUCHer.net

To:

vOUCHer

From:

www.OUCHer.net

Spend time together

How spending time together can help

As humans, we are sociable beings who like to spend time with other people. At other times we may need to be alone. When we listen to ourselves we know which one we need.

Sometimes we may miss people we care about. The time we spend without them can be painful. These times can cause us to feel unsettled, nervous, distressed or another negative emotion.

Connecting with that person can help us feel calmer and increase our confidence.

> *"Spending time with you is so precious and I love every minute that we are together."*

#6 Replacement password: 104729

VOUCH!

This voucher asks the receiver to spend some time with me.

I have drawn how I am feeling

VOUCH!

This voucher asks the receiver to spend some time with me.

I have drawn how I am feeling

To:

vOUCHer

From:

www.OUCHer.net

To:

vOUCHer

From:

www.OUCHer.net

Be Patient

How being patient can help

By being shown patience and space we can give ourselves the opportunity to find our own solutions.

Sounds, movement, thoughts and emotions all create energy waves, but for any wave to be generated it needs space. Imagine a butterfly in a cacoon trying to fly. There would be no space for it to take flight.

What patience can give us is the space to allow thoughts and feeling to fulfil their purpose of being thought and felt. Patience can help us remove the cocoon and to spread our wings for us to move towards our full potential.

Have patience. All things are difficult before they become easy.

Saadi

#7 Replacement password: 658302

VOUCH!

This voucher asks the receiver to listen patiently to me. Something has happened that has made me feel:

I have drawn how I am feeling

VOUCH!

This voucher asks the receiver to listen patiently to me. Something has happened that has made me feel:

I have drawn how I am feeling

To:

vOUCHer

From:

www.OUCHer.net

To:

vOUCHer

From:

www.OUCHer.net

Speak without judgement

How non-judgement can help

Nobody has spent their whole lives with another person, except us with ourselves. Even as babies we had our own unique thoughts, feelings, experiences and perspectives whilst being born and sleeping alone at night.

For this reason, it is said that we can never know enough to judge another person. It is impossible to know what each person has fully experienced in their whole life and why someone may have behaved the way they did.

When a person is not judged they can feel accepted for who they truly are. Instead of being judged and labelled, they can feel that the person they are speaking to is coming from a place of empathy and compassion in trying to understand the situation from their point of view.

Be curious, not judgmental.

Walt Whitman

#8 Replacement password: 079183

VOUCH!

This voucher asks the receiver to listen to me. I have a problem for which I need some non-judgemental advice based on what you might do if you were in my position.

I have drawn how I am feeling

V

VOUCH!

This voucher asks the receiver to listen to me. I have a problem for which I need some non-judgemental advice based on what you might do if you were in my position.

I have drawn how I am feeling

V

To:

vOUCHer

From:

www.OUCHer.net

To:

vOUCHer

From:

www.OUCHer.net

Take a look

How receiving honest feedback can help

Asking for and receiving honest feedback can help us to conclude our own thoughts and feelings.

When hearing feedback, we sometimes know instantly, in our heart or stomach, if the person's opinions or advice is right for us moving forward.

Other peoples' opinions and advice can help us to see situations and even life in a new way.

It takes strength and courage to admit the truth.

Rick Riordan

#9 Replacement password: 452769

VOUCH!

This voucher asks the receiver to look at something and give me their honest advice about:

a. Something online
b. School work
c. My body
d. My diary entry
e. Other: ____________________

VOUCH!

This voucher asks the receiver to look at something and give me their honest advice about:

a. Something online
b. School work
c. My body
d. My diary entry
e. Other: ____________________

To:

vOUCHer

From:

www.OUCHer.net

To:

vOUCHer

From:

www.OUCHer.net

I would like to listen

How learning from others experiences can help

Other people's stories can help us realise that everybody experiences difficult times and feelings at some point in their life.

Listening to how that person got through a tough time can help us learn useful ways to support ourselves through our own difficulties.

The discoveries and lessons learnt from other peoples experiences can, should you wish, be passed on to others to help them through their own emotional challenges.

I am still learning.

Michelangelo at aged 87

VOUCH!

This voucher asks the receiver to tell me:

a. An embarrassing story from when you were my age
b. Your biggest fear when you were my age
c. Your biggest regret when you were my age
d. If you could go back in time, what advice would give yourself at my age

VOUCH!

This voucher requests that the receiver tells me

a. An embarrassing story from when you were my age
b. Your biggest fear when you were my age
c. Your biggest regret when you were my age
d. If you could go back in time, what advice would give yourself at my age

To:

vOUCHer

From:

www.OUCHer.net

To:

vOUCHer

From:

www.OUCHer.net

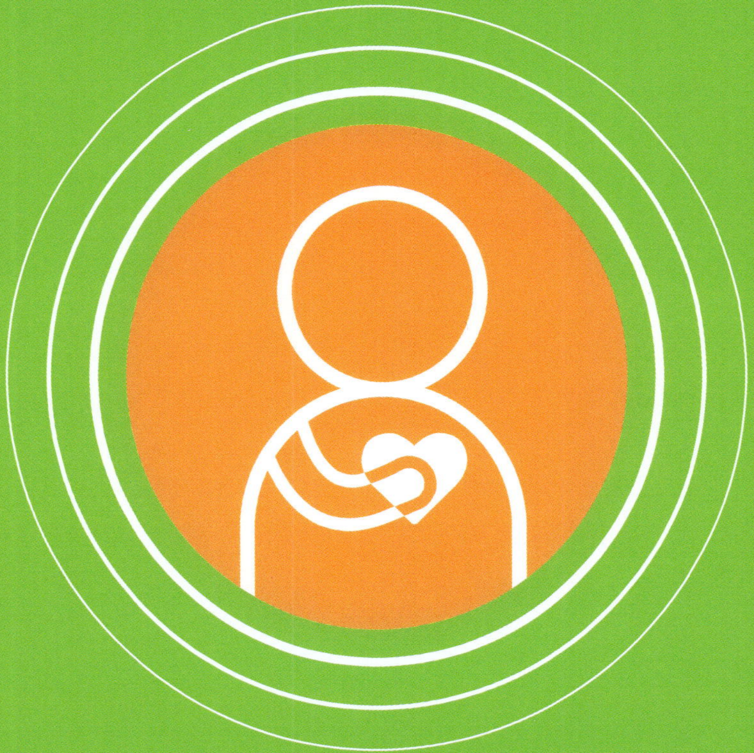

Clarifying

How clarifying can help

Getting more than one opinion before deciding your own view can help you have peace of mind. Knowing that you have heard a broad range of views can help you feel more confident about your decision.

Understanding your own views can help you develop your next step by giving you the purpose, courage and confidence to do so.

Clarifying also demonstrates maturity, by realising that different views can help you extend your knowledge to make an informed choice that is best for you.

> *The discipline of personal mastery starts with clarifying the things that really matter to us & living our lives in the service of our highest aspirations.*
>
> Peter Senge

#11 Replacement password: 128794

VOUCH!

This voucher asks the receiver to tell me the truth. Someone said: ______________________

____

____

Is this true?

VOUCH!

This voucher asks the receiver to tell me the truth. Someone said: ______________________

____

____

Is this true?

To:

vOUCHer

From:

www.OUCHer.net

To:

vOUCHer

From:

www.OUCHer.net

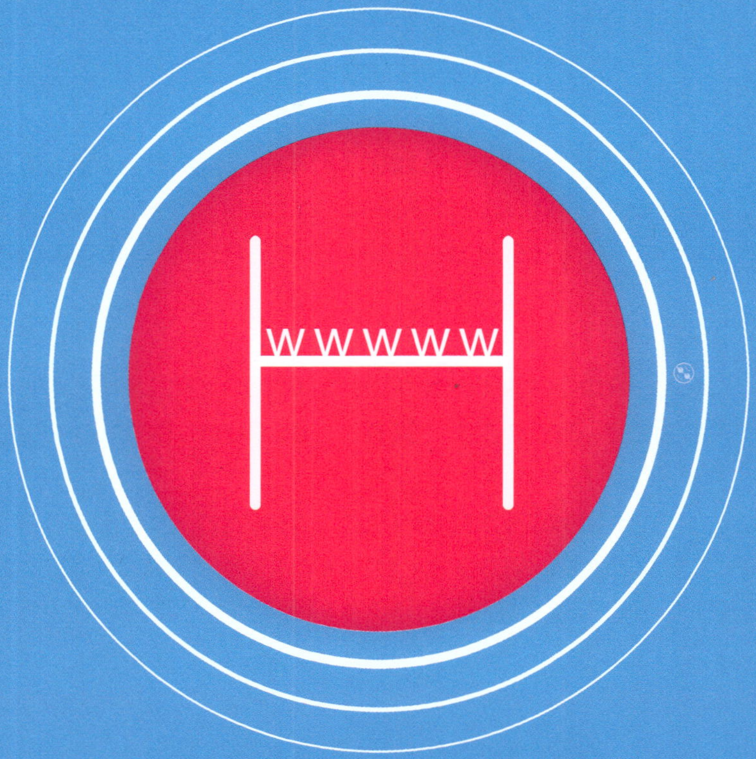

I have a question

How questioning can help

Asking questions can help us to find a new view of the world. This can support us in life and help us with the difficulties it can bring.

Finding and asking questions of other people can be a fantastic way to expand our own understanding, knowledge and views on many different topics.

If you are wondering what to ask, remember the 5 birds sat on a rugby post (see the icon above). The H shaped rugby post is the **How** and the 5 birds are the W's of **What**, **When**, **Where**, **Who** and **Why**!

> *Even though there are no ways of knowing for sure, there are ways of knowing for pretty sure.*
>
> Lemony Snicket

#12 Replacement password: 072945

VOUCH!

I have a question: ______________________________

VOUCH!

I have a question: ______________________________

To:

vOUCHer

From:

www.OUCHer.net

To:

vOUCHer

From:

www.OUCHer.net

Additional support

For those times you are unsure who to speak to, there are organisations that can offer you support, should you wish to contact them.

Samaritans

If you need someone to talk to, we listen. We won't judge or tell you what to do.

116123

jo@samaritans.org

www.samaritans.org

Childline

A free, private and confidential service where you can talk about anything.

0800 1111

www.childline.org.uk

Kooth

Free, safe and anonymous online support for young people. Kooth can be someone to understand or to offer advice when you need it.

www.kooth.com

Shout

24/7 UK crisis text service available for times when people feel they need immediate support.

www.giveusashout.org

Text 85258

Young Minds

Leading the fight for a future where all young minds are supported and empowered, whatever the challenges.

0808 802 5544

www.youngminds.org.uk

Calm Harm

Calm Harm is an app developed for teenage mental health charity stem4 by Dr Nihara Krause it uses an evidence-based therapy called Dialectical Behavioural Therapy (DBT).

www.calmharm.co.uk

Crisis

Crisis is the UK national charity for homeless people. The charity offers year-round education, employment, housing and well-being serviceshomeless.

www.crisis.org.uk

LGBT Foundation

LGBT Foundation is a national charity delivering advice, support and information services to lesbian, gay, bisexual & trans communities.

0345 3 30 30 30

www.lgbt.foundation

Mindfulness NHS

Paying more attention to the present moment – to your own thoughts and feelings, and to the world around you – can improve your mental wellbeing. You can check your mood using this simple mood self-assessment quiz.

www.nhs.uk/conditions/stress-anxiety-depression/mindfulness/

About the creators of vOUCHers

Jennifer Dunning

Having initially worked in the care sector supporting children, Jennifer now works in education with a particular interest in special educational needs.

From both at work and volunteering with Samaritans, Jennifer is acutely aware of the impact trauma and emotional turmoil can have on everyday life. Jennifer believes that by developing a network of support and talking about these issues we can move towards feeling and ultimately easing our difficult emotions.

Markus Baker

With his first career as a nursery nurse along with Markus' current one as a visual communicator creates a perfect mix for unique ideas to come to life.

Markus has a broad view of society. This comes from his many experiences that include designing for the film industry, volunteering for Samaritans, qualifying as a psychotherapist and travelling the world, which included staying with a Taoist Master in the hills of South Korea.

vOUCHers

Did you spot Sam hiding on every page and vOUCHer in this book? If you didn't it is ok because Sam was not supposed to found until you were aware.

Look at Sam's face and tilt your head to your right and then tilt your head to the left. It is the same face but one looks happy and from the other angle it looks sad.

Sam's face represents that sometimes a situation does not change, but how we see it does.

Each of the vOUCHers and pages in this book can help you develop a different view and way of looking at your life.

Jennifer and Markus hope you enjoyed this book and that you found it helpful. If you would like to tell us what you think about this book, please do so at www.OUCHer.net

Printed in Poland
by Amazon Fulfillment
Poland Sp. z o.o., Wrocław

62658706R00037